OUTSIDE
AND
INSIDE
TREES

by

SANDRA MARKLE

SCHOLASTIC INC.

New York Toronto London Auckland Sydney

For Fred and Kathleen Wagner
Good friends are the real roots of any family tree

With special thanks to Dr. R. Bruce Hoadley,
Dr. Thomas O. Perry, and Dr. Judy Morgan,
and Dr. M. Eloise Brown Carter
for sharing their invaluable expertise,
assistance, and enthusiasm

*Copyright © 1993 by Sandra Markle.
All rights reserved. Published by Scholastic Inc., 555 Broadway,
New York, NY 10012, by arrangement with Bradbury Press,
An Affiliate of Macmillan Publishing Company.
Printed in the U.S.A.
The text of this book is set in Melior.
Book design by Christy Hale.
ISBN 0-590-48952-6*

2 3 4 5 6 7 8 9 10   14   01 00 99 98 97 96 95 94

*Note to parents and teachers: To help young readers pronounce
words that are likely to be unfamiliar, a pronunciation guide is
presented on page 35. The first appearance of these words is
italicized in the text. For children who might like to know
exactly how many times the magnified images have been
enlarged, this information can be found with the photo credits
at the back of the book. The symbol × after the number
means "times."*

Like you, trees are special living things. Do you ever wonder what's inside? Or how a tree lives and grows? This book will let you take a peek and find out.

4

The bark is smooth on a young pine, but as the tree grows older and bigger, the bark splits into overlapping plates.

The bark is a good place to start. Just as your skin protects your body, the tree's bark protects what's inside. It shields against heat and cold. It keeps the tree from drying out. It keeps out insects, which might damage the tree. It helps keep *bacteria* and *fungi* out, too. Bacteria and fungi are living things. Most bacteria and fungi are harmless, but some are not. If harmful bacteria and fungi get inside, they can make the tree sick.

Bark isn't stretchy like skin, though. If there is a big tree nearby, look at its bark. Is it wrinkled? Is it peeling? That's what happens as the tree grows bigger around. Luckily, the cracks on a healthy tree are never deep enough to break completely through the bark.

The whole tree, including the bark, is made up of cells. Cells are like tiny building blocks. There are leaf cells, wood cells, root cells, and bark cells—special cells for every part of the tree. Many of the pictures in this book were taken with the help of a tool called a *microscope*. Through a microscope, it's easy to see that bark is made up of layers of cells.

Look at the close-up picture of bark. A kind of fatty material has separated the outer bark cells from their supply of water and food. This causes the outer bark cells to die. Little by little, the outermost layers of bark flake off. New cells are constantly growing, though, adding on new, living layers of inner bark. Unless it's damaged, a tree's bark will never become too thin to protect it.

outer bark   inner bark   sapwood

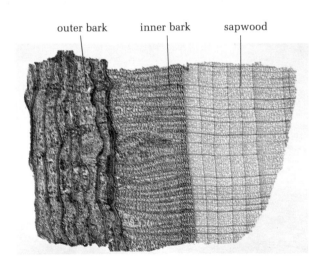

Bark is so well sealed that air can reach the living cells only through small holes. These holes, called lenticels, look like dots or dashes and are usually only easily seen on smooth bark.

Alaskan cedar

sycamore

A tree's bark is a good place to start if you want to find out if a tree is an oak, a maple, or some other type of tree. What is one way in which the bark in the first picture is different from the others? Each type of tree has its own special bark pattern. But trees that are the same type tend to look very similar.

redwood

oak

7

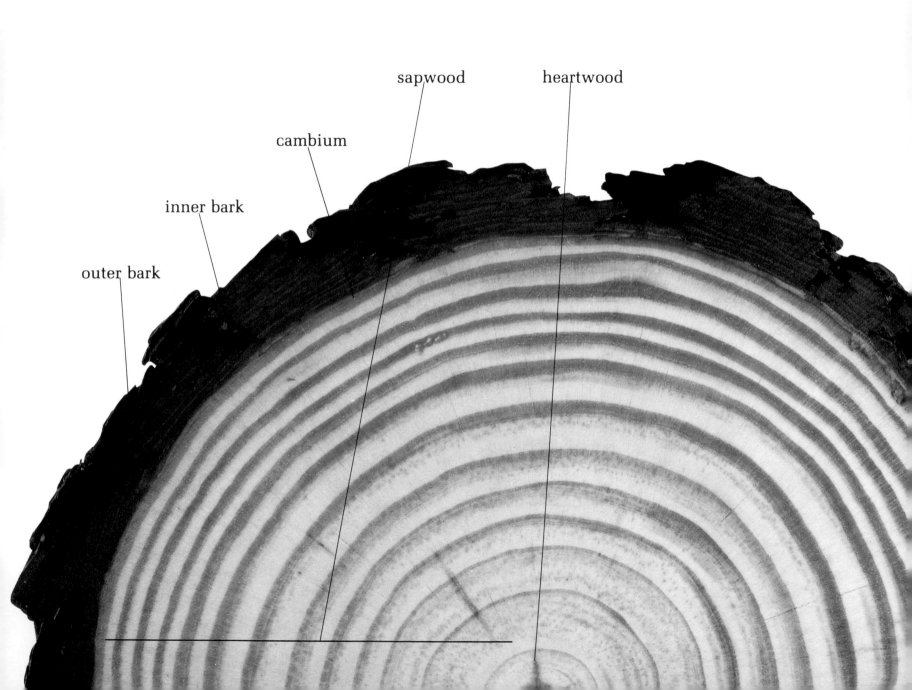

sapwood

heartwood

cambium

inner bark

outer bark

Now that you've taken a close look at a tree's bark, what's under it? The tree's trunk is one big plumbing system.

Find the inner bark, or *phloem*, in the picture. It's made up mostly of tubes. They carry sugar from the leaves and branches to supply all parts of the tree with the energy it needs to live and grow.

Now look for the sapwood, or *xylem*, which makes up the whole middle of the trunk. The sapwood is full of another kind of tube. These tubes carry water and tiny bits of matter from the soil, called minerals, up from the roots to the branches and leaves.

Do you see the heartwood in the very center of the tree? This is formed when the innermost layers of sapwood cells die as a natural part of a tree getting older. Oils and a gummy material may plug the sapwood tubes. And together, all the plugged tubes form a strong, hard core for the tree.

There's another, paper-thin layer of cells sandwiched between the outer edge of the sapwood and the inner bark. This special layer, called the *cambium*, produces the new sapwood cells toward the inside of the tree, and new inner bark cells toward the outside of the tree.

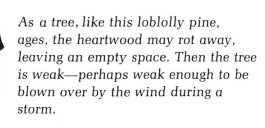

As a tree, like this loblolly pine, ages, the heartwood may rot away, leaving an empty space. Then the tree is weak—perhaps weak enough to be blown over by the wind during a storm.

Sapwood cells produced in the spring usually have thinner walls than those produced during the summer and fall. Thicker walls help make the tree strong enough to support its heavy crown of leaves, flowers, and seeds or fruit.

Because of the thinner cell walls, wood produced in the spring usually looks lighter than the wood that's produced later. Together, one year's set of early and late wood rings form an annual ring. Counting annual rings in a tree that has fallen or been cut down shows about how many years a tree lived. Look back on page 8. About how many years old was that tree?

This boy is blowing bubbles through a piece of red oak whose end was dipped in liquid dishwashing soap. No hole was drilled in the wood, so how could he do it?

In some hardwoods, like red oaks, the sapwood tubes are like long straws formed by cells stacked end to end. The bottom and top of each cell have melted away so all the cells are joined.

Trees are sometimes divided into two groups by their type of wood—hardwoods, like oaks, and softwoods, like pines. Hardwoods have many more thick-walled cells than softwoods do. Also, the cells are more tightly packed together in hardwoods.

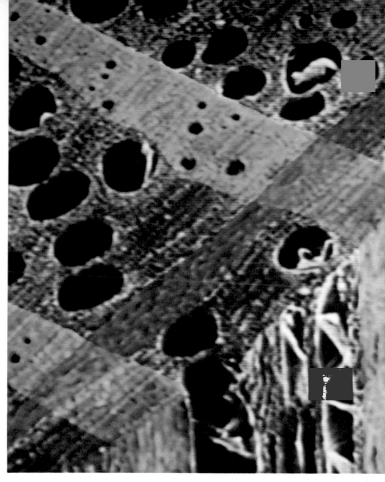

color enhanced and magnified
This close-up look lets you see that wood isn't as solid as it feels. The holes are the tops of tubes formed by sapwood cells. In some trees, like maples, all the sapwood tube openings are about the same size. In others, like this oak, the tubes formed in the spring have bigger openings.

A tree's roots often extend a lot farther out from the trunk than the tree's longest branch—as much as seven times farther. When trees are close together, feeder roots from a number of different trees will crisscross each other, competing for the available water and minerals.

This tree's roots have been exposed and painted white so you can see them easily.

Some trees, such as oaks, tend to have a few strong, deep taproots, which help the tree stand up straight and anchor it in the ground. Other trees, like poplars, have many tough, shallow roots that do the same job. But all trees have a network of thin feeder roots, which fan out just below the surface of the soil. The job of these roots is to collect the water and minerals the tree uses to make food. They also take in oxygen, a gas in the air. The tree's cells combine the oxygen with the tree's sugar-food to produce energy.

Don't be fooled. The white fuzzy threads you can see in this picture aren't tiny roots. They are a special kind of helpful fungi. When fungi come into contact with a tree's roots, they push into the tree's cells. Then they collect water, minerals, and oxygen from the soil and pass them along to the tree. In return the tree shares its sugar-food with the fungi.

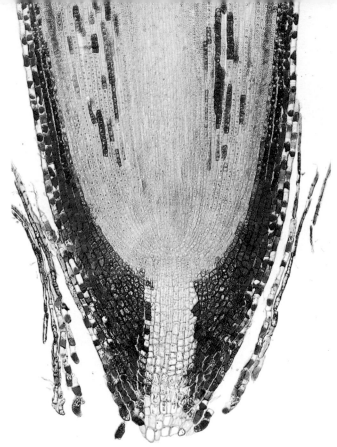

color enhanced and magnified
This is a root tip. A tree's roots are constantly growing longer. As this happens, the tip is pushed forward. Some outer cells drop off, forming a slippery surface that helps make it easier for the root to push through the soil.

Here you can see the fungi, as thin as hairs, that grow out beyond the root tips.

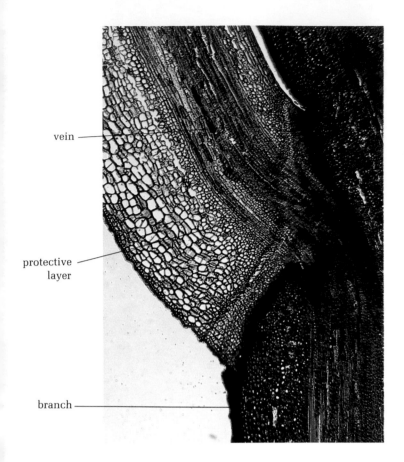

vein

protective
layer

branch

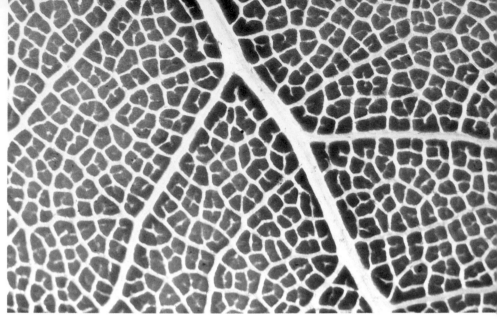

leaf veins

color enhanced and magnified
*See the dark band across the base of
the stem? This shows that the leaf is
about to drop off the tree. A fatty
material has built up in a layer of
cells at the base of the leaf stem. This
will seal the branch so there won't be
a hole when the leaf breaks away.*

Now, here's something you can see without special equipment. Hold a leaf and look at the many thin lines running through it. Those are veins. This close-up picture lets you see that the veins become smaller and smaller, so they can get close to all the leaf's cells.

Next, peek inside this maple leaf's stem. You can see that these veins connect the leaf to the tree's sapwood and phloem tubes. It's no wonder that losing a whole section of branches and leaves may cause some of a tree's roots to die. Or that when part of the root system dies, part of the tree's crown of branches and leaves will die, too.

14

Tree leaves come in many different sizes and shapes. They may be broad and flat, like oak leaves, or slender rods, like pine needles. They may be made up of only one part, or divided into small leaflets, like the leaves on a buckeye tree. Like bark patterns, leaf shapes can be used to tell if a tree is a sycamore, a mountain ash, a gingko, or one of the many other tree types.

pine

An oak's leaves are arranged so that they spiral around the branch. This growth pattern helps sunlight reach every leaf.

Pine leaves are shaped like needles. This compact shape and a thick, waxy coat protect the needle-leaves from cold, dry weather.

oak

buckeye

While one big leaf might tear in the wind, the group of leaflets forming the buckeye's leaf just flutters.

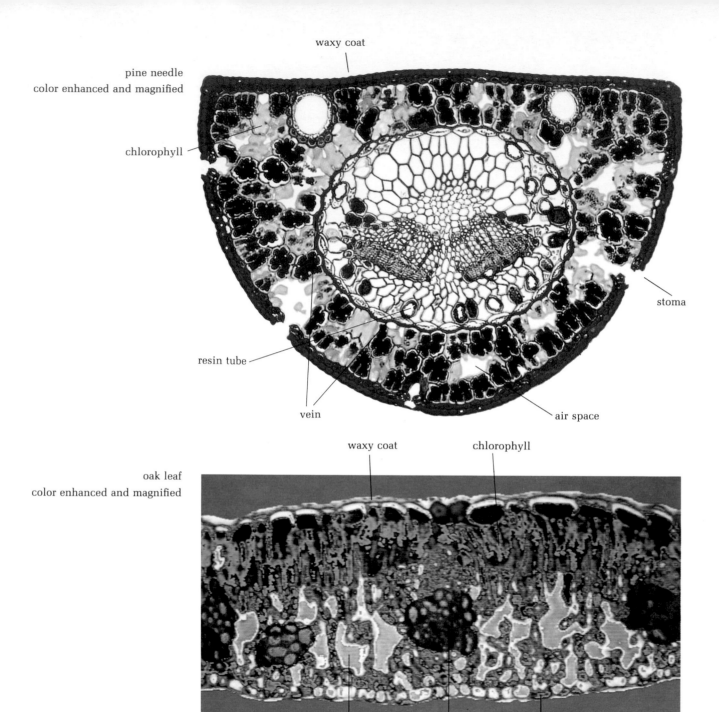

waxy coat

pine needle
color enhanced and magnified

chlorophyll

stoma

resin tube

vein

air space

waxy coat   chlorophyll

oak leaf
color enhanced and magnified

16

air space   vein   stoma

You have to buy your food at a grocery store or gather it from a garden. But a tree makes the food it needs through a process called *photosynthesis*. Its food is a special type of sugar called *glucose*. Glucose is made mainly in the leaves, but some trees also make it in their twigs and branches.

No one has been able to figure out exactly how a tree makes food. But scientists know that it can happen only when there is the green coloring matter called *chlorophyll*, as well as water, *carbon dioxide* gas, and sunlight. Chlorophyll absorbs the sun's light energy and changes it into a special form of chemical energy the tree can use. Then, in a way that is still a mystery, this energy drives a process that uses water and carbon dioxide to produce glucose. Oxygen is given off as waste during this process. But that's lucky for animals and people, who need to breathe oxygen to live.

Pine needles and oak leaves are different in other ways besides their shapes. Pine needles have tubes filled with a special gummy substance, called resin. This is what you smell when you crush pine needles. While oak leaves are shed every fall, pine needles remain on the tree for many years. Pine needles also continue to produce food during the winter, except when temperatures drop below freezing.

See how this tree has its longest branches near its base? Can you guess how this helps sunlight reach every leaf on the tree?

Cutout shapes, like those on oak leaves, also help light reach all the tree's leaves. Swaying and fluttering keep leaves in the sunlight, too.

stoma, open   color enhanced and magnified   stoma, closed   color enhanced and magnified

The stomata open when the guard cells take in water, swell, and bend apart.
They close when the guard cells lose water, shrink, and press together.

Leaves get the supply of carbon dioxide they need to make food right from the air. Air enters the leaves through tiny openings called *stomata*, which are no bigger than pinpoints, bordered on either side by guard cells. Carbon dioxide in gas form can't pass through a cell's protective wall, though. First, it must mix with water because water can pass through easily. To keep all the leaf cells supplied with water, the stomata also control the flow of water through the tree.

When the stomata are open, very tiny droplets of water escape into the air. Water droplets have a natural attraction that makes them stick together. So, as some water goes into the air, it pulls on the water still inside the leaf. This, in turn, pulls on water in the sapwood tubes. Like a chain of people holding hands, this pull tugs the water upward through the tree. As water leaves the roots, more water is drawn into the tree.

19

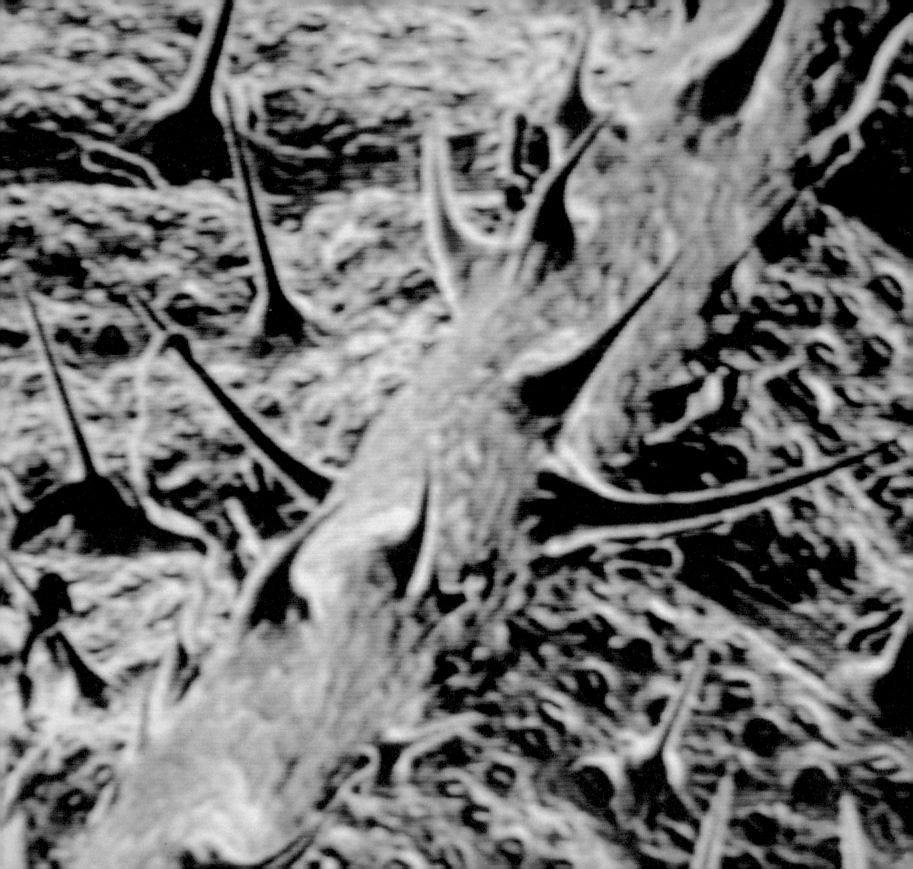

You may wonder how the pull of water droplets leaving tiny holes in a leaf could make water rise clear to the top of a tall tree. This close-up picture shows that a leaf's surface is nearly covered with stomata. Just imagine how many openings there must be on a tree's whole crown of leaves!

There are tiny holes on the twigs, too. The combined pull of water leaving the tree through so many openings is a strong force. It's enough to make water rise even to the top of a tree giant.

color enhanced and magnified

What look like dots are stomata. Tree leaves usually have most of their stomata on the lower surface. This keeps the sun's heat from making the leaf lose water too quickly. Some leaves, like this one, also have tiny hairs. These probably slow airflow over the leaf and help keep it from drying out.

This is a leaf scar, the spot where the branch was sealed before the leaf fell off. Find the tiny dots on the scar. Those are the sealed ends of the leaf's veins. Just above the leaf scar is the developing bud that will produce the next leaf.

Red shades, like those of the sugar maple in this picture, develop after the leaf stem is sealed. These beautiful colors are produced when the sugar trapped inside the leaf breaks down.

Leaves that seem to turn bright yellow, brown, and shades of orange in autumn really contained those colors all the time. These shades were just masked by the bright green chlorophyll in the leaf cells. In autumn, as hours of daylight grow shorter, food production slows down. Then less new chlorophyll is made. Since chlorophyll breaks down during food production, the green color in the leaf gradually disappears. At last, you can see the leaf's secret colors.

Leaves that fall continue to help the tree. As the fallen leaves rot, minerals are returned to the soil and can be used by the tree to produce more leaves.

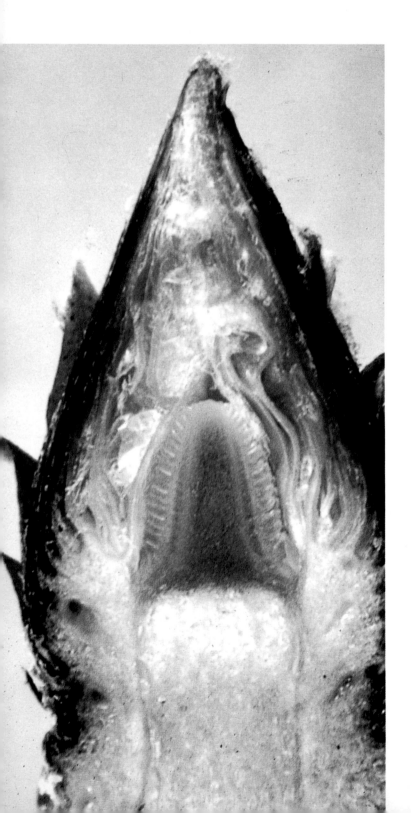

magnified
In the very center of this Douglas fir tree bud, you can see the tiny beginning of what will be the new, longer stem.

Waxy, overlapping scales on the outside of the bud protect the leaves from cold winds, rain, and snow.

Trees also may be grouped by the way they shed their leaves. Some, like maples, lose all their leaves in autumn. Others, like pines, drop only a few leaves at a time all year long. But even trees that shed their leaves all at once aren't really bare during the winter. New leaves are already forming, tucked safely inside buds.

Look closely at buds on different trees. Like leaves and bark, buds can help people who study trees tell one type from another.

In the spring, as the days grow longer and warmer, a new supply of water is drawn into the roots. This carries the tree's stored food up through the phloem tubes in the trunk and branches to the buds, where it supplies energy for growth. Buds at the tips of branches begin to grow first. Besides new leaves, these buds produce the new shoots that will make the branches longer.

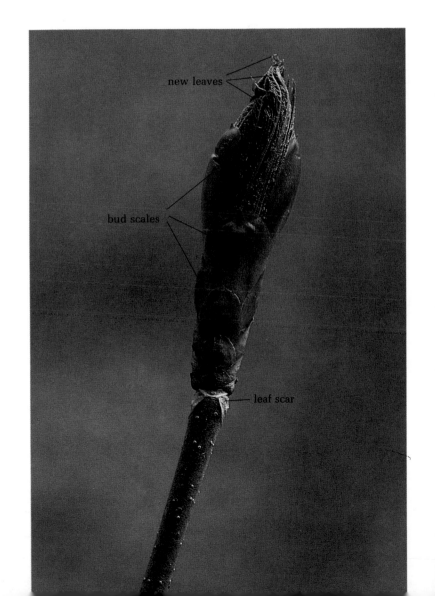

new leaves

bud scales

leaf scar

The brown band around this branch is a scar made when the bud scales of the end bud dropped off. Find rings like this on a branch. Measure from the tip of the branch to the first ringed bud scale scar you find. That's how much the branch grew this year. Now look farther down the branch to find rings of bud scale scars from other years. Did the branch grow more one year than another?

As the new shoot pushes out, the hard bud scales separate and fold back. At first, the young leaves are small, pale, and folded. Then the shoot lengthens and the leaves open and grow bigger. No longer needed, the bud scales drop off, leaving a scar that encircles the branch. Chlorophyll production quickly starts, turning the leaves green.

Have you ever seen a tree in bloom? Tree flowers are also produced by the buds. Some tree flowers, like those of the magnolia, are very beautiful and easy to spot. Others, such as those of the red maple, are small and may not look much like flowers to you. But whatever they look like, tree flowers have an important job. They produce seeds, the life packages from which new trees will grow.

Tree flowers have male and female parts. On magnolias, they are together on the red stalk in the center of the flower. On red maples, they are grouped in separate clusters of male and female flowers.

red maple female flowers

magnolia

red maple male flowers

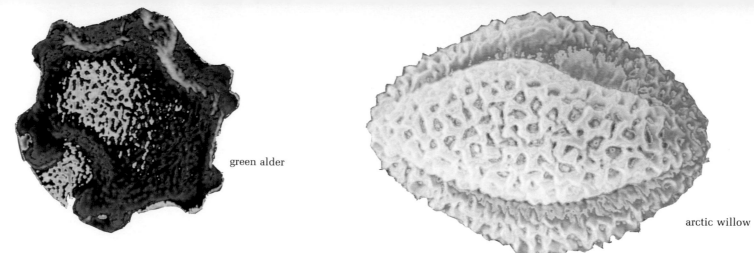

green alder

arctic willow

These strange-looking things are tree *pollen*, produced by the male flower parts. But don't worry. Each pollen cell is really as tiny as a bit of dust. In the spring, when there is lots of pollen in the air, you may see it as a yellow coating on cars and puddles.

Pollen may be carried by the wind, by insects such as bees, by hummingbirds, or by bats. Trees that depend on animals to carry their pollen usually have flowers that are easy to see. They often produce a sweet juice called *nectar,* which attracts the animals.

The top of the female part of the flower is sticky. Each pollen grain that sticks to this part sends a tube down to an egg cell. The pollen cell and the egg cell unite, forming an *embryo,* or a young plant capable of becoming a new tree. The embryo, plus a supply of stored food and any protective coat, becomes a seed.

shortleaf pine

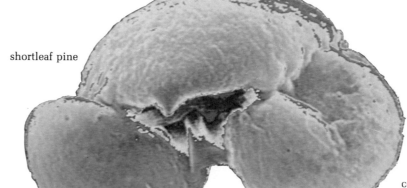

color enhanced and magnified

Pines, spruces, and firs produce pollen and eggs in separate cones. When the embryos are fully developed, the cones fall apart. Each seed has a papery wing so it can ride away on the wind.

Some types of pines also produce special cones that remain on the tree for many years. These cones only open if the tree is burned in a forest fire or damaged in some way. Then the seeds quickly scatter and sprout to start new trees growing.

The embryo, which will sprout and grow into a new pine tree, is in the center. Around it is a supply of stored food that will give it the energy it needs to start growing.

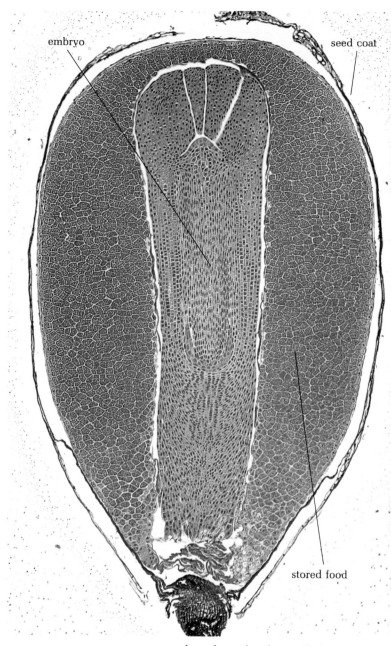

embryo

seed coat

stored food

color enhanced and magnified

This is a mature seed cone. The egg-bearing cones are much bigger than the pollen-bearing cones, and they remain on the tree for about two years, as the seeds develop.

Squirrels like to eat acorns, so they collect and bury lots of these tree seeds to store for the winter. Can you guess what happens to the acorns they don't dig up and eat?

Maple seeds have papery "wings" and fly away on the wind.

acorns, or oak seeds

samara, or maple seeds

You probably won't be surprised to learn that each type of tree produces its own special type of seed. You may have even eaten some. Nuts are tree seeds. And you can look for tree seeds inside many fleshy fruits, such as apples, cherries, and peaches.

Some seeds, like those of the willow, have a bit of fluff to carry them away on the wind. Apples are eaten by animals, but the seeds have a hard coat to keep them from being digested. The seeds pass out with the animal's droppings. Coconuts are light enough to float and are waterproof. They often sail away on ocean waves.

Seeds need to escape from the parent tree. Being on their own gives the young trees room to spread their roots and branches so they can grow big and tall.

Most seeds leave the parent tree in the fall. But they don't begin growing until spring. As the soil warms and water from spring rains or melting snow reaches the seed, the embryo's cells become active. New cells are quickly produced. The root pushes out of the seed first. Then the stem and first leaves stretch up into the sunlight. At first, food stored in the seed supplies the young tree with energy. But it soon begins to produce its own food.

This little redwood sprouted from a seed no bigger than the thickness of a nickel. It's most likely to be damaged by disease, by insects, or even by a poor supply of water during its first year. If it survives, it may live for hundreds of years.

Imagine what it would be like if you only grew taller from the top of your head and the tips of your toes. That's the way a tree grows taller— from the tips of its branches and roots.

How tall you'll get to be usually depends on the traits you've inherited from your family. That's true for trees, too. A full-grown dogwood tree is usually much shorter than a full-grown oak tree. Giants, like these coastal redwoods, grow to be over three hundred feet tall. That's as tall as a thirty-story building!

Trees are beautiful to look at. But even more importantly, trees add a lot to life on earth. They supply food, oxygen, homes for many animals, and even the basic building materials for houses. Every part of a tree has a job that helps keep the tree alive. And all of its parts work together, so a tree can make food, transport water, and produce leaves, flowers, and seeds. Little or big, a tree is a special living thing from the inside out.

To help support their increasing height, all trees grow about an inch bigger around every year. Redwoods, like these, are not only giants among trees, they're among the tallest living things on earth.

PRONUNCIATION GUIDE

BACTERIA   bak tir′ ē ə

CAMBIUM   kam′ bē əm

CARBON DIOXIDE   kär′ bən dī äk′ sīd

CHLOROPHYLL   klôr′ ə fil′

EMBRYO   em′ brē ō′

FUNGI   fun′ jī

GLUCOSE   glōō′ kōs

LENTICELS   len′ ti səls

MICROSCOPE   mī′ krə skōp′

NECTAR   nek′ tər

OXYGEN   äk′ si jən

PHLOEM   flō′ em

PHOTOSYNTHESIS   fōt′ ə sin′ thə sis

POLLEN   päl′ ən

RESIN   rez′′n

STOMATA   stō′mə tə

XYLEM   zī′ ləm

GLOSSARY/INDEX

in the soil, attaches to a tree's roots, supplying the tree with water and minerals. In return the tree supplies the fungi with food. **5, 13**

GLUCOSE: A type of sugar produced by trees during photosynthesis. **17**

HARDWOODS: Trees, such as oaks, whose wood is mainly made up of small, thick-walled cells that are tightly packed together. **11**

HEARTWOOD: The center portion of the tree's sapwood, which forms as the innermost layers of sapwood cells die. **8–9**

LATE WOOD: The wood produced by the tree from the end of the spring through the remainder of the tree's growing season. **10**

LEAF SCAR: The mark left on the stem when the leaf falls off. **22**

LEAVES: The usually green, broad, flat, or needle-shaped part of a tree that is mainly where glucose, a type of sugar, is produced. These may be simple, meaning there is only one leaf to a stem, or compound, meaning there are a number of leaflets to a stem. **9–10, 14–26, 31–32**

LENTICELS: Openings through the bark, which allow oxygen and tiny droplets of water to exit and carbon dioxide to enter. They look like dots or dashes. **6**

MICROSCOPE: An instrument that uses a lens or a combination of lenses to make very small things look bigger. **6**

MINERALS: The nonliving materials in the soil that a plant needs to grow and be healthy. Those considered the most important are carbon, potassium, calcium, magnesium, nitrogen, phosphorus, sulfur, and iron. **12–13, 23**

NECTAR: Sweet liquid produced in flowers to attract insects and animals. When the animals and insects brush against the male, pollen-producing part of the flower, some sticks to their bodies. Then, if they move on to another flower of the same type of plant, the pollen is carried to the female part of the flower. When the male and female parts join, a seed is formed that is able to produce a new plant. **28**

OXYGEN: This gas that animals need to breathe in order to live is given off as waste during photosynthesis. A tree does use some oxygen, though, during the process that breaks down sugar and yields energy for the tree to grow. **12–13, 17**

PHLOEM: The tubes that transport sugar through the tree. **9, 14, 25**

PHOTOSYNTHESIS: The process in which chlorophyll changes the sun's light energy to chemical energy. This energy is used to produce glucose from carbon dioxide and water. The tree's leaves are the main site of photosynthesis. Trees that lose their leaves in the fall still carry on photosynthesis as long as the temperature is above freezing. Bare twigs and branches that contain chlorophyll continue to make food. This food is stored until the tree begins to actively grow again. **17**

POLLEN: Produced by the male part of a flower, this contains the male cells, or sperm. **28–29**

RESIN: A clear, yellowish to brown semistiff liquid produced in cone-bearing trees, such as pines. It is most often produced if the tree is injured, and it helps protect it from decaying and from being attacked by insects. **16–17**

ROOTS: These are a very important part of the plant, because they both anchor the plant in the soil and absorb water and minerals. See **taproots** and **feeder roots. 9, 12–14, 19, 24–25, 30–31**

SAPWOOD: The name given to the living tubes that carry water up through the tree. These tubes are also called the xylem. **8–11, 19**

SEEDS: These are formed when a female egg cell and a male sperm cell unite. They produce new plants. Some trees must be quite old before they start to produce seeds. An oak, for example, is usually fifty years old before it produces acorns. Then an oak may produce as many as 50,000 acorns in a year. **27–32**

SOFTWOODS: Trees whose wood cells are mainly large and thin-walled. This term is commonly used to mean the wood of cone-producing trees, such as pines. **11**

STOMATA (stoma, singular): Openings the size of pinpoints, bordered by guard cells, through which carbon dioxide enters the leaf and oxygen and tiny water droplets exit. **19–20**

TAPROOTS: The main, deeper roots that help anchor the tree in the ground. **12**

TRUNK: The woody stem of the tree. **9**

VEINS: A bundle of tubes carrying water and minerals to a leaf's cells and carrying away the sugar produced there. The veins also form the supporting framework for the leaf. **14, 16, 22**

XYLEM: Special tubes that transport most of the water and minerals throughout the tree. **9, 14**

PHOTO CREDITS